# HANGZHOU

# 杭 州

FOREIGN LANGUAGES PRESS   BEIJING

外文出版社 北京

# HANGZHOU

Hangzhou, described as "the most beautiful and luxurious city in the world" by the noted Italian traveler Marco Polo in the 13th century, is a leading historical, cultural and tourism city in China, as well as the capital of Zhejiang Province.

Located 150 kilometers southwest of Shanghai, the famous metropolis in southeast China, Hangzhou was one of the birthplaces of Chinese civilization, as well as one of the country's six ancient capitals. As early as 50,000 years ago, the "Jiande People" lived here. Hangzhou people, together with those living in the Taihu Lake Valley, created the famous "Liangzhu Culture" 4,700 years ago. In the 3rd century, Sun Quan, from Hangzhou's Fuyang County, established the Kingdom of Wu (222-280) in southern China, which was one of the Three Kingdoms, together with Shu and Wei. In the 7th century, Emperor Yangdi of the Sui Dynasty (581-618) linked Beijing and Hangzhou by means of the Grand Canal, laying a solid foundation for the prosperity of Hangzhou. In the 10th century, Qian Liu, from Hangzhou's Lin'an County, founded the Kingdom of Wuyue in southeast China, making Hangzhou its capital. In the 12th century, Emperor Gaozong of the Northern Song Dynasty (960-1127) was defeated and escaped to southern China, establishing the Southern Song Dynasty (1127-1279). Emperors Kangxi (1662-1722) and Qianlong (1736-1795) of the Qing Dynasty (1644-1911) traveled along the Grand Canal from Beijing to inspect Hangzhou five and six times, respectively, in consideration of Hangzhou's important role in the nation's economy and culture. This long history of the city has left a rich cultural heritage. At present, Hangzhou has six sites of cultural relics under the special protection of the State and 58 under the protection of the province.

Hangzhou enjoys beautiful natural scenery, with numerous tourism resources including the West Lake and the Fuchun River-Xin'an River (Thousand-Island Lake), two national-grade scenic areas; Mount Tianmu and Qingliang (Cool) Peak, two national nature reserves; Thousand-Island Lake, the Fuchun River, Mount Daqi and Mount Wuchao, four national-grade forest parks; the Zhijiang National Tourism Resort; the Qiantang River Bore, a rare scene in the world; and the famous Beijing-Hangzhou Grand Canal. In addition, there are 10 national scenic spots, five national nature reserves and 35 provincial scenic spots around Hangzhou.

The West Lake in Hangzhou is known as a classical example of traditional landscape culture, full of elegant, natural and harmonious concepts of traditional Chinese culture. The West Lake contains historical, religious, landscaping, natural resources and art treasures, integrating the essence of Hangzhou culture. Over 100 scenic spots, including 10 spots at the West Lake, Lingyin Temple, Yue Fei's Temple and the Pagoda of the Six Harmonies, are scattered in the 60-sq-km area.

The Fuchun River-Xin'an River (Thousand-Island Lake) scenic area, known for its green mountains, clear rivers, secluded environment and long history, boasts many scenic spots, including Stork Mountain, Tongjun Mountain, Yan Ziling Fishing Terrace, Meicheng Old Town, Hanging Temple of Great Mercy Rock and Hai Rui's Memorial Temple, which were already popular tourist sites 1,000 years ago. In the Tang Dynasty (618-907) over 100 noted poets, including Li Bai, Meng Haoran, Bai Juyi, Liu Changqing, and Du Mu, left many famous poems in those places. Poets of successive dynasties all left behind here beautiful examples of poetry and prose, making the 200-kilometer scenic belt a typical oriental landscape culture tour route. This route is also called the "Golden Tour Route of West Zhejiang" because it is linked with the famous Mount Huangshan.

The Qiantang River Bore is a world-famous natural wonder. Viewing the bore has become a tradition among the people of Hangzhou. At the same time, the old Grand Canal linking Beijing and Hangzhou is rich in cultural and folklore connotations.

Mount Tianmu is known for its primitive forests. It was the place where Zhang Daoling, a leading Taoist of the Eastern Han Dynasty (25-220), was born and cultivated himself to reach spiritual perfection. It then became a sacred land of Buddhism, with many scholar monks living there. Its influence spread as far as Japan and Southeast Asia The exotic rocks and stones, green streams and deep ponds, tall old trees, and temples are well worth visiting.

All tour routes in Zhejiang Province are centered on Hangzhou. The East Zhejiang Province Route from Hangzhou to Ningbo and Zhoushan via Shaoxing integrates water-township culture, Tang poetry culture and Buddhist culture. In Shaoxing, one may find old towpaths, black-awning boats, Keqiao Town, Keyan Scenic Spot, the East Lake, Dayu's Mausoleum, Lanting Pavilion, Shen's Garden, Three-flavor Reading Room, Yinshan Tomb and Jianhu Lake, forming the cultures of boat, bridge, stone, wine, calligraphy and scholarship. Lingyin, Tianzhu and Jingci temples in Hangzhou, Tiantong, Ayu and Baoguo temples in Ningbo, and Puji, Fayu, Huiji temples on Putuo Island are historical relics of Buddhism in southeast China, and still attract believers. The aquatic tour route from the West Mausoleum of Hangzhou to Linhai via Shaoxing, Shangyu, Xinchang and Tiantai is the earliest birthplace of the school of landscape poetry in China as well as the famous "Route of Tang Poetry in Eastern Zhejiang Province." The famous Mirror Lake, Dayu's Mausoleum, Ruoye Brook and King Yue's Terrace, together with the Kuaiji, Siming, Tianlao, Chicheng and Tiantai mountains, are beautiful natural scenery. The Hemudu Culture Ruins of 7,000 years ago are located in Yuyao, Ningbo.

Since Zhejiang borders on the East Sea, the east coast of the province is an aquatic tour route, embracing Putuo Mountain, the Shengsi Islands and Shenjiamen Fishing Harbor.

Tiantai Mountain, Yandang Mountain, the Nanxi River and Xiandu Mountain are four national-grade scenic resorts on a famous tour route called "Beautiful Mountains and Rivers of Southern Zhejiang Province." The route stretches from Ningbo to Taizhou, Weizhou and east of Lishui. Tiantai Mountain boasts many natural and historical sites. Guoqing Temple on the mountain is the birthplace of the Tiantai Sect, the first sect of Buddhism in China, with a history of over 1,400 years. In addition, Tiantai Mountain is the birthplace of the Southern Sect of Taoism in China. Yandang Mountain, known as a "Museum of Topography," has exotic peaks, winding streams and waterfalls. The Nanxi River scenery, stretching over 150 km, includes pure water, elegant mountains, exotic rocks and beautiful forests. There are many buildings and villages dating from the Song, Ming and Qing dynasties. According to a legend, Xiandu Mountain is the place where the Yellow Emperor made pills of immortality and went up to Heaven.

The Central Zhejiang Province Tour Route, centered on Jinhua, is full of the mythical color of Chinese culture. The national-grade underground river, Double-dragon Cavern, Jinhua Temple, Square Rock Mountain and Zhuge Liang's Eight Trigrams Village can all be found here. The farmers of Dongyang, in this area, have built the Hengdian Film and TV City.

Hangzhou, together with Huzhou and Jiaxing in the north, is called the Hangjiahu Area, and is known for its water-towns, for being a home of fish and rice, a home of silkworms and one of the birthplaces of silk civilization in ancient China. Nanxun, Xitang, Wuzhen and Xinshi are famous silk towns. Mao Dun, Wu Changshuo, Feng Zikai, and Qian Juntao, famous literati or artists, were all born in this area.

Some nature reserves under the protection of the State and the province such as Fengyang Mountain, Baishanzu Mountain, Wuyan Peak, Gutian Mountain and Nine Dragons Mountain in Quzhou and Lishui to the southwest of Hangzhou compose the Ecological Tour Route. Other attractions are the Southern Confucius Temple, Longyou Grottoes, ruins of Longquan Kiln, folklore of  the  She people and the Longquan sword production technique.

Museums in Zhejiang provide plenty of information for tourists to get to know more about local history and culture. The Zhejiang Museum, Zhejiang Natural History Museum, Chinese Tea Museum, Chinese Silk Museum, Official Kiln Museum of the Southern Song Dynasty and Hu Qingyu's Drug Store Museum in Hangzhou; Yueju Opera Museum in Chengzhou; Chinese Huzhou Brush Museum in Huzhou; and Zhoushan Museum in Zhoushan all display the historical and cultural achievements of Hangzhou and Zhejiang. Dragon boat races, fishermen's wedding, worship of Dayu, folklore of the She people, viewing the moon and appreciating flowers are all living aspects of the local cultural traditions.

# 杭　　州

　　杭州，这个被13世纪意大利著名旅行家马可·波罗誉为"世界上最美丽华贵之城"的地方，位于中国东南部著名大城市上海西南150余公里处，是中国著名的历史文化名城和重点风景旅游城市，也是浙江省的省会。

　　杭州历史悠久，是华夏文明的发祥地之一和中国六大古都之一。早在5万年前，这里就有"建德人"居住。4700多年前，杭州与太湖流域先民共同创造了著名的"良渚文化"。公元三世纪，杭州富阳人孙权在中国江南建立了吴国（公元222－280年），与蜀、魏两国三分中国的天下。公元七世纪，隋炀帝将运河从北京接通到杭州，为杭州的繁荣发达奠定了深厚的基础。十世纪，杭州临安人钱镠又在中国东南部建立了吴越国，并建都杭州。十二世纪，宋高宗败退江南，在杭州定都建立了南宋王朝（公元1127－1279年），历时150年。十七至十八世纪，鉴于杭州经济、文化在全国的重要地位，清帝康熙（公元1662－1722年在位）、乾隆（1736－1795年在位）祖孙两代都分别5次和6次从北京沿运河巡视到杭州。悠久而重要的历史为杭州留下了丰富的历史文化遗产，使其至今拥有飞来峰石刻造像等6处国家级文物保护单位与钱王陵等58处省级文物保护单位。

杭州风光秀丽，旅游资源极为丰富。拥有西湖和富春江——新安江（千岛湖）两个国家级风景名胜区、天目山和清凉峰两个国家自然保护区、千岛湖、富春江、大奇山、午潮山等四个国家级森林公园和之江国家旅游度假区，并拥有举世罕见的钱塘江大涌潮和著名的京杭大运河等胜景，在杭州周围还有10个国家级风景名胜区与5个国家级自然保护区、35个省级风景名胜区。

杭州西湖远古时只是一个"泻湖"，千百年来，人们在对它进行加工建设之中，注入了中国传统文化的理念，使之具备了开合得宜、秀雅柔和、自然自在、中庸平和等诸多品质，并成为中国传统山水文化的经典。不仅如此，西湖的文化博大精深，其所蕴含的古迹文化、宗教文化、园林文化、物产文化、艺术文化、名人文化等文化现象散落在60平方公里的山山水水之间，几乎囊括了杭州文化的最精华部分，并形成了西湖十景、灵隐寺、岳庙、六和塔等近百处著名景点。

富春江——新安江（千岛湖）景区以"山青、水清、境幽、史悠"为特色，拥有著名的鹳山、桐君山、严子陵钓台、梅城古镇、七里泷、大慈岩悬空寺、海瑞祠等古老的山水与文化名胜，早在1000多年以前已成为热门的风景名胜旅游线，唐朝（公元618－907年）时李白、孟浩然、白居易、刘长卿、杜牧等百余著名诗人行吟其间，留下了许多脍炙人口的名诗，使之成为名副其实的"浙西唐诗之路"。其后的历代诗人，也都在此留下了数以千计的优美诗文，使这一长达二百公里的风光带，成为典型的东方山水文化旅游线。此线还与中国著名黄山相连，称之为浙西黄金旅游线。

钱江潮是世界著名的自然奇观，钱江观潮是杭州人持续千百年来的习俗，人们在钱塘江边祭潮、观潮、诵潮、建造镇潮物和海塘大提，形成了全国独有的潮文化。同样，从京城贯通到杭州的古运河，也孕育了杭州运河两岸从生产方式、建筑形式到民风民俗等方面的独特文化。

西天目山以"高、大、古、稀、多、美"为特色的原始森林景观，与其宗教名山的历史是相辅相成的。此处传为东汉（公元25－220年）道教宗师张道陵的出生地与修道地，以后又长期成为佛教圣地，高僧辈出，影响远及日本及东南亚。其奇岩怪石、碧溪深潭、古木大树、寺殿古迹等景观殊为丰富。

以杭州为中心的浙江诸多旅游线，也无不充满独特的文化色彩。从杭州沿绍兴至宁波、舟山的浙东旅游线，荟萃了最具中国特色的水乡文化、唐诗文化和佛教文化景观。绍兴水乡拥有古纤道、乌蓬船、柯桥、柯岩、东湖、大禹陵、兰亭、沈园、三味书屋、印山大墓、鉴湖等船文化、桥文化、石文化、酒文化、书法文化和名士文化的丰富景观。杭州的灵隐、天竺、净慈等寺庙与宁波的天童寺、阿育王寺、保国寺、以及舟山普陀岛的普济、法雨、慧济等大寺，是中国"东南佛国"的历史遗迹，至今仍香火不绝。而从杭州萧山西陵起始，经绍兴、上虞、新昌、天台直到临海的水上旅游线，是中国最早的山水诗派的发祥地，又是著名的"浙东唐诗之旅"线。其间著名的镜湖、禹陵、若耶溪、越王台、剡溪、沃洲等名水名迹与会稽、四明、天姥、赤城、天台等名山，至今犹充满诗情画意。宁波余姚还有著名的七千年前的"河姆渡文化"遗址。

浙江东部濒临东海，因此浙东沿海又是一条海洋旅游线，其间除了著名的普陀山外，还有国家级风景名胜区嵊泗列岛、百岛县洞头、大渔港沈家门等，蕴含着中国古老的海防文化、渔业文化、佛教文化等丰富文化内涵。

由宁波南下至台州、温州和丽水东部是著名的浙南奇山秀水线。沿途有天台山、雁荡山、楠溪江、仙都山等四个国家级风景名胜区。天台山千峰竞秀，万壑争流，景色幽奇，名人踪迹多多。其国清寺是中国佛教第一个宗派天台宗的发源地，已有1400多年历史。此外，天台山还是中国道教南宗祖庭。雁荡山峰峦奇特、溪瀑神奇，有"地貌造型博物馆"之称。楠溪江全长150公里，水清、山秀、岩奇、滩林美，更有众多宋、明、清古建筑和古村落，可品读古代"耕读世家"和"宗族社会"的概貌。仙都山传为中华民族始祖轩辕黄帝炼丹升天处，山不高而奇，水清且幽。

以金华地区为主的浙中旅游线，则充满中国文化的神奇色彩。这里有国家级风景名胜区地下长河、岩溶奇观双龙洞，还有道家传说人物黄大仙得道处"金华观"、民间传奇人物胡公大帝的圣地——方岩山、中国古代著名的智囊人物诸葛亮的后裔聚居之地——兰溪诸葛八卦村等。此地，古民居荟萃，在建筑之乡东阳，还有一座农民兴办的"横店影视城"。杭州与其北部的湖州、嘉兴是统称杭嘉湖地区。杭嘉湖是中国著名的水乡、鱼米之乡与蚕乡，中国古代丝绸文明的发祥地之一。这里有丝绸古镇南浔、西塘、乌镇、新市等，并孕育了中国近代著名的文学家、艺术家茅盾、吴昌硕、丰子恺、钱君匋等。

杭州西南的衢州、丽水两市境内有凤阳山、百山祖、乌岩岭、古田山、九龙山等众多国家级与省级自然保护区，构成了一条生态旅游线。在优美的生态环境中，还珍藏着南孔庙、龙游石窟、龙泉窑遗址等古迹与畲家少数民族风情和古老的龙泉宝剑生产工艺。

杭州及其所在的浙江，不愧是美丽的山水之地与精彩的文化之邦。要历史地了解其各方面的文化现象，还可以走进它拥有的众多的博物馆。在杭州的浙江博物馆、浙江自然博物馆、中国茶叶博物馆、中国丝绸博物馆、南宋官窑博物馆、胡庆余堂博物馆和嵊州的越剧博物馆、湖州的中国湖笔博物馆、舟山的舟山博物馆等，形象生动地展示了杭州和浙江的历史文化成就。而至今保存在各地的龙舟竞渡、渔民婚礼、公祭大禹、畲乡风情、赏月赏花等民俗活动，则是历史遗存的活文化。

杭州及周边地区旅游交通图
Map of Places in and around Hangzhou

The southern part of the Beijing-Hangzhou Grand Canal, where waterways crisscross this "home of fish and rice" and center of China's silk industry. Hangzhou is located at the southern end of the canal.

京杭大运河江南段、河道成网、风光秀丽、是中国的鱼米之乡、丝绸之府、文化之邦。杭州就位于它的终端。

The people of Zhejiang were pioneers of traditional Chinese culture.

浙江大地，人杰地灵，人文荟萃。人们在这里，创造了广泛而经典的中国传统文化。

Chenghuang Pavilion is a new building by the West Lake in Hangzhou.

城隍阁，杭州西湖世纪末的建筑。

Baoshu (Bless and Protect Hongshu) Pagoda, constructed 1,000 years ago, is a landmark of the West Lake.

建于 1000 年前的保俶塔秀美挺拔，有"保俶如美女"之喻，正是西湖风景的标志之一。

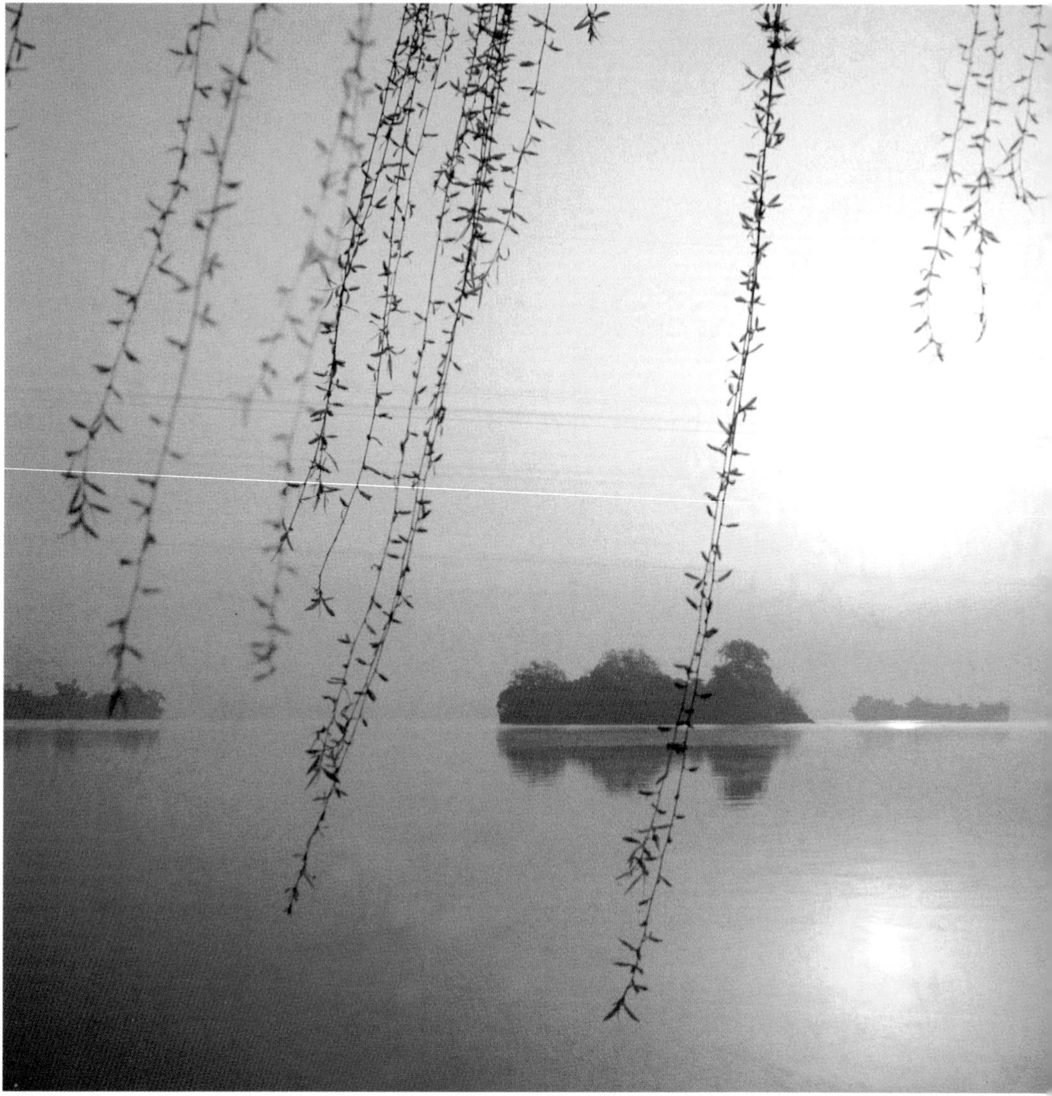

## The West Lake

The West Lake is a national-grade scenic resort, covering an area of 60
square kilometers. It was a gulf in ancient times and turned into a lagoon
after silt blocked the mouth of the gulf. Since the Tang Dynasty (618-
907), the lake has been dredged several times, and causeways and
islands have been constructed. At present, the Bai Causeway and Su
Causeway separate the lake into the Outer Lake, Inner Lake, Yuehu
Lake, Xili Lake and Small South Lake, with some natural and artificial
islets in the middle. There are altogether 100 scenic spots in the area,
including five spots with cultural relics under special state protection,
10 spots on the West Lake and 10 spots on the New West Lake, plus
hills, springs, caverns, temples, gardens and historical sites.

## 西湖

为国家级风景名胜区，总面积60平方公里，其中湖面5.6平方公里，
周长15公里，远古时为海湾，后因泥沙淤积，封闭海湾口，形成泻
湖。唐朝以来，人们按照传统文化理念对其进行了不断的改造、浚湖、
筑堤、建岛等。现主要有白堤、苏堤，把湖面分割成外湖、里湖、岳
湖、西里湖和小南湖。湖中有天然岛屿孤山和人工岛屿小瀛洲、湖心
亭、阮公墩。全景区有风景名胜百余处。其中有国家文物保护单位5
处、西湖十景、新西湖十景及名山、名泉、名洞、名寺、名迹、名园
等景观。

### Spring on the West Lake

In spring, tulips, azaleas and peonies blossom. Peach and willow trees are planted along the causeways of the lake.

### 西湖之春

西湖之春是花的世界，湖堤两旁间栽桃树与柳树，因此，古人吟西湖诗中有"一株杨柳一株桃"的句子，此外，还有郁金香、杜鹃、牡丹花等各种花卉展现其间。

### Snow on the Broken Bridge

The Broken Bridge is the starting point of the Bai Causeway. When it snows, the scene is especially beautiful. The Legend of White Snake, a folk love story, is supposed to have taken place here.

### 断桥残雪

断桥位于白堤的起点。断桥雪景、空灵晶莹、清心净性。描写人蛇之恋的民间故事《白蛇传》中的男女主人公就是从这里开始演绎了一段美丽的故事。

## Three Pools Mirroring the Moon

One of the ten scenic spots on the West Lake, the three stone pagodas stand in the lake. On the night of the Autumn Moon Festival, three candles are lit in the hollows of the three pagodas. The light of the candles is reflected in the lake, forming the scene of "one moon in the sky, three shadows on the lake."

### 三潭映月

为西湖十景之一，三座石塔立在湖中，塔身中空呈球形。中秋之夜，塔内点烛，封以薄纸，烛光倒映湖中，形成"天上月一轮，湖中影成三"的奇景。

19

### Snow Scene on Chuyang Terrace
Chuyang Terrace is located on the highest point of Geling Peak in the north of the West Lake, serving as an ideal place to view the sunrise and the snow scenery.

### 初阳台雪景
初阳台在西湖北山葛岭最高处，为观日出和雪景的最佳之处。

### Spring on Small Yingzhou Islet
Small Yingzhou Islet was built of silt after dredging the lake, dividing it into four squares by bridges and causeways, forming a unique scene.

### 小瀛洲春色
小瀛洲为浚湖之泥所筑，岛中湖面被桥堤分割成"田"字形，构成湖中有岛，岛中有湖，风光独绝的景观。

**Princes Park**

This is the place where two princes of the Southern Song Dynasty (1127-1279) were buried. It was later opened as a park where an annual tulip fair is held.

太子湾公园

旧为南宋庄文、景献两太子葬地，后辟为公园，原始质朴。每年在此举办郁金花展。

**The Temple of the Soul's Retreat**

Built in 326, the Temple of the Soul's Retreat is one of the ten famous temples in China. The Hall of the Great Deity, 33.6 meters high, built in the Qing Dynasty (1644-1911) but in Tang Dynasty (618-907) style, is the best-preserved temple of one layer and two eaves in the domestic area. The sculpture inside the Hall of the Heavenly King is carved out of a whole piece of camphor wood, a relic of the Southern Song Dynasty.

灵隐寺

建于公元326年，为中国十大名刹之一。其大雄宝殿为清光绪末年所建仿唐建筑，高33.6米，是国内保存最好的单层重檐三叠寺院建筑。天王殿内的韦陀雕像系用整块香樟木雕成，为南宋遗物。

### Grottos on the Peak That Flew Here

This is a site of cultural relics under special state protection. There are over 470 stone statues on cliffs, dating from the Five Dynasties, Song Dynasty and Yuan Dynasty (10th -14th centuries). They are rare artistic treasures in southern China.

### 飞来峰石窟

为全国重点文物保护单位。各洞壑和岩壁上雕有五代、宋、元（约在公元 10-14 世纪）石刻造像470 多尊，是江南少见的石窟艺术瑰宝。

### ◁ Nine Brooks and Eighteen Dales

Located 10 kilometers southwest of the West Lake, this place boasts many beautiful natural scenes.

### 九溪烟树

位于西湖西南十余公里处的九溪十八涧，溪涧横流，景观野逸。清学者俞樾（公元1821-1907年）赞之为："重重叠叠山，曲曲环环路，丁丁东东泉，高高下下树。"

### Song Dynasty City

The Song Dynasty (960-1279) City was the first theme park in Hangzhou, as well as the biggest park with the theme of Song culture in China. It reproduces the scenes on the long scroll titled *Market at the Pure Brightness Festival*, a famous painting of the Song Dynasty.

### 宋城

杭州第一个主题公园，也是全国最大的宋文化主题公园，生活化地展示了宋代名画《清明上河图》所描绘的场景及宋朝民俗风貌。

## Official Kiln of the Southern Song Dynasty (1127-1279)

This is the largest ancient pottery kiln site in southern China. Beside the kiln, there is a small-sized oven, a reproduction of an official kiln, and the Official Kiln Museum of the Song Dynasty.

### 南宋官窑遗址

为中国南方最大的古窑遗址保护建筑，有龙窑和制瓷作坊遗迹。遗址旁建有小型仿官窑炉和南宋官窑博物馆。

**Pagoda of the Six Harmonies**

The King of Wuyue constructed this pagoda in 970. The octagonal pagoda, made of bricks with seven layers inside and 13 layers outside, is under special state protection.

六和塔

建于公元970年、吴越王为镇江潮而建。砖结构木檐外廊、八面，内七层外十三层。为全国重点文物保护单位。

## Hu Qingyu's Drug Store

This was built in 1874 by Hu Xueyan, a wealthy businessman of the Qing Dynasty (1644-1911). It integrates the advantages of residential houses and gardens of southern China with rational structure, fine materials, exquisite engravings and luxurious decorations. The store is in the front, and the workshop is behind, serving as a rare example of a business building of the Qing Dynasty. It is now under special state protection. Part of the building is a museum of traditional Chinese medicine.

胡庆余堂

系清朝巨商胡雪岩于1874年创办的中药店，其建筑集江南住宅园林之长，布局合理，用材讲究，雕刻精致，装饰华丽，是国内难得的清代前店后坊式商业建筑，为全国重点文物保护单位。部分建筑辟为中药博物馆。

### Viewing the Bore at Haining

The Qiantang River Bore is a wonder of the world. In olden times, people viewed the bore from the Pagoda of the Six Harmonies in Hangzhou. Now it is viewed from Haining, 40 kilometers east of the pagoda.

### 海宁观潮

钱江潮为世界奇观，由太阳与月亮引力和钱江入海口特殊地形造成。古时观潮在杭州六和塔，现东移至 40 多公里外海宁。此处动态观潮，可见"碰头潮"、"一线潮"、"回头潮"等诸多形态，蔚为壮观。

## Mogan Mountain

Mogan Mountain, a national-grade scenic spot 60 kilometers from Hangzhou, is one of the four largest summer resorts in China. Its "three wonders" are bamboos, clouds and springs, and its "four treasures" are green, clean, cool and calm.

## 莫干山

距杭州60公里，为中国四大避署胜地之一、国家级风景名胜区，有竹、云、泉"三胜"，绿、净、凉、静"四宝"。

### ◁ East Lake

The East Lake is a famous scenic spot of Shaoxing, 60 kilometers from Hangzhou. It was formed from a Han Dynasty (206BC-A.D.220) quarry. It became famous at the end of the Qing Dynasty (1644-1911) as a park, with rocks, caves, bridges and lakes.

### 东湖

距杭州60公里绍兴的名胜，为汉代（公元前206－220年）因采石造就的残山剩水，清末辟为园林，岩、洞、石、桥、湖巧妙结合，成为名湖。

### Dayu's Mausoleum

The area contains Dayu's Tomb, Dayu's Memorial Hall and Dayu's Temple. Dayu is said to have tamed floods and harnessed rivers in ancient times. His festival is held in the third month by the lunar calendar.

### 大禹陵

传为夏禹陵墓，由禹陵、禹祠、禹庙三部分组成，依山临水，高低错落，气势雄壮。1995年始每年农历三月初有隆重祭禹活动。禹是中国传说中的古代部落联盟领袖，因治水除患，受人民敬仰。

### Ancient Towpath

Connecting Xiaoshan Hill and the canal at Shaoxing, these stone slabs were laid over 1,000 years ago. The path, the bridge, the water and the boat are in harmony, just like a picture.

### 古纤道

萧山至绍兴运河岸畔的 一大奇观，以石板架设水上、连以石桥，作古代纤夫背纤行舟之用，有千年历史，构思奇特，路、桥、水、船浑然一体，美妙如画。

### Water Lane at Keqiao

Keqiao, known for its stone bridges and water lanes, is steeped in the folklore of Shaoxing. It is the largest old district of Shaoxing, which is famous for its wine, and textile goods market.

### 柯桥水巷

柯桥为绍兴最大古镇，黄酒酿造中心，现又为著名轻纺市场。柯桥以石桥与水巷著称，呈典型的绍兴风情。

**Houshan Hill**

Located in the eastern suburbs of Shaoxing, the hill was a quarry 1,000 years ago. It is famous for its grotesque rocks, and fascinating springs and caverns.

吼山

在绍兴市东郊，1000多年前因采石成此残石妙景。现有底小顶大的云石、棋盘石等惊险巨石，还有烟萝洞、云泉等水景。

## Exotic Rock

This was part of a quarry 1,000 years ago, and is 30 meters high. The cypress tree on the top is over 1,000 years old. The Giant Buddha Rock beside it was carved by three generations of artisans, and was completed in the 4th century.

### 柯岩云骨

为千余年前采石残留的奇景, 高30余米, 顶端古柏树龄达千年, 人称为"绝胜"。其旁有大佛岩, 大佛相传雕于公元4世纪, 由三代工匠相继雕刻而成。

**Jianhu Lake at Shaoxing**

It is said that the Yellow Emperor once threw a mirror into this lake, hence the name "Mirror Lake." The water is of high quality, and is used to make the famous Shaoxing rice wine. The lake is rich in aquatic products, and pearl breeding is a popular occupation.

绍兴鉴湖

周围近百里，相传黄帝曾铸镜于此，故又名"镜湖"。其水质极佳，绍兴黄酒专用此水酿成。湖中水产丰富，亦养殖珍珠。

### Tianyi Pavilion

Constructed in the 1660s, Tianyi Pavilion is the oldest library in China. It is under special state protection.

### 天一阁

建于 16 世纪 60 年代，为中国现存最古老的藏书楼，珍藏善本丰富，为全国重点文物保护单位。

42

## 宁波三古寺

天童寺为中国佛教禅宗五山之第二，已有1600多年历史，规模宏大，环境幽深，珍藏宋以来文物殊多，亦为日本佛教曹洞宗祖庭。阿育王寺建于公元282年，因珍藏释迦牟尼真身舍利子而闻名中外。保国寺至今已有970多年历史，为中国江南幸存的最古老最完整的木结构半拱建筑，全部构件皆用榫卯技术巧妙衔接，不用一钉一铆。大殿的梁架被天花板和镂空的藻井巧妙遮住，故有"无梁殿"之称。

## The Three Old Temples of Ningbo

The Tiantong Temple is a well-known Buddhist temple with a history of over 1,600 years. It is large in scale and has a quiet environment, presening many cultural relics of the Song Dynasty (960-1279). The King Ayu Temple, constructed in 282, is famous for its remains of Sakyamuni. The Baoguo Temple is the oldest and best-preserved wooden and half-arched building in southern China, with a history of over 970 years. The whole structure is linked with mortise and tenon joints, and not a single nail was used during its construction. The beams of the hall are concealed, giving it the name "Beamless Hall."

**Pantuo Rock on Putuo Mountain**

The three characters on the rock were written by Hou Jigao, a noted military official of the 16th century. In 1916, Dr. Sun Yat-sen came here and wrote "Rock of the Soul."

磐陀石

为普陀山一景。"磐陀石"三字系 16 世纪抗倭名将侯继高所写。1916 年孙中山到此一游，题字"灵石"二字。

◁ **Moonlight on the Zhoushan Archipelago**

Zhoushan is one of the three largest fishing ports in the world. It is rich in tourism resources, including state-level and provincial-level scenic spots such as Putuo Mountain, the Shengsi Islands, famous temples, exotic rocks and golden sand.

舟山群岛月色

舟山为世界三大渔场之一，全市有普陀山、嵊泗列岛、朱家尖等国家与省级景区，有名刹、奇岩、金沙、渔港等丰富旅游资源。

### Sand Sculpture Festival at Zhoushan

This annual festival is held on the 5-kilometer golden sand beach at Zhujiajian, On the Zhoushan Archipelago. Dozens of professional sand sculpture teams come to participate. Tourists may join in the competition.

舟山沙雕节

在舟山朱家尖十里金沙滩上举行。1999年为首届，而后每年举行。届时国内外有数十支专业沙雕队参赛，游客在此可看沙，玩沙和做沙雕。

## Shitang at Wenling

Shitang is a famous fishing harbor, with Shitang Mountain in the north, and the sea in the southeast. It was the place where Chinese people welcomed the dawn of the new millenium. Most of the buildings are made of stone.

## 温岭石塘

北倚石塘山，东南面海，为著名渔港，最早迎接世纪曙光之处。其建筑多用石料,石屋、石墙、石路，依山就势，自成一格。

**Floating on the Nanxi River**

The Nanxi River is a national-level scenic spot with 36 bays and 72 beaches.

**楠溪江漂流**

楠溪江为国家级风景名胜区，江水清且深，有"三十六湾七十二滩"，为漂流胜地。

◁ **Hezhang Peak on Yandang Mountain**

Yandang Mountain, known for its fantastic peaks, exotic stones, waterfalls and springs, is one of the ten famous mountains in China. Hezhang Peak, in the shape of two palms placed together before the breast, presents different shapes when viewed from different angles.

**雁荡山合掌峰**

雁荡山为中国十大名山之一，以奇峰怪石，飞瀑流泉著称。其峰峦移步换形，此合掌峰从不同角度又依照其形取名为夫妻峰、双乳峰、雄鹰峰、相思女等。

## Thousand-Island Lake
This huge artificial lake was formed after the Xin'an River Hydropower Station was constructed, covering an area of 580 square kilometers and having 1,078 islets.

### 千岛湖
为新安江水电站筑坝拦江所形成的巨大人工湖，面积580平方公里，有1078个岛屿。碧水清澄，旷秀清新，有梅峰观岛、五龙岛、海瑞祠等胜景。

### The Fuchun River

The Fuchun River, known as "a unique landscape in the world," boasts beautiful scenery. The section between Meicheng and Qililong is the most elegant part of the river.

### 富春江七里扬帆

富春江山水奇秀，古人称"富春山水、天下独绝"。自梅城下舟至七里泷，"无风七里，有风七十里"，形容船借风势，行驶迅急。此处又是富春江风光最奇秀的江段。

## Yan Ziling's Fishing Terrace

The terrace is located near Qililong on the Fuchun River. Yan Ziling, a good friend of Emperor Liu Xiu of the Eastern Han Dynasty (25-220), lived here in seclusion. Yan Ziling refused Liu Xiu's offer of a court post and enjoyed farming and fishing at Fuchun Mountain for the rest of his life.

## 严子陵钓台

位于富春江七里泷附近，为严子陵隐居处。严子陵为东汉（公元25-220年）光武帝刘秀同窗好友，刘秀多次召其出仕辅政而不受，终生隐居富春山中，甘以耕钓为乐。

### The Hanging Temple of Southern China
Located on the Rock of Great Mercy in Jiande, the temple is suspended from a cliff, 147 meters high and with a brook running under it.

### 江南悬空寺
位于建德大慈岩，古寺半入岩腹，半凌空，与山西省恒山悬空寺异曲同工。主峰巨岩为天然立佛，高147米。岩下有壮观的长谷溪流。

## Hai Rui's Memorial Temple

Located on Longshan Island in Chun'an, the former temple sank into the lake. The present one was constructed in 1985. Hai Rui (1514-1587) who served as the head of Chun'an County, was upright, just and honest, and was greatly admired by the local people.

### 海瑞祠

筑于淳安千岛湖龙山岛上。海瑞（公元1514－1587年）曾任淳安知县，清正廉洁，为民崇敬。原祠已沉入湖底，此为1985年重建。

### West Tianmu Mountain

This is a national-grade nature reserve, with sturdy ancient trees. The mountain has many Taoist and Buddhist scenic spots, including Chanyuan Temple, Prince Temple and Qianzhang Cliff.

### 西天目山

为国家自然保护区，林木以"高、大、古、稀"著称。此山又是中国道教与佛教胜地，有禅源寺、太子庵、千丈岩等景点。

### Hengdian Film and TV City

Hengdian in Dongyang is a national model township enterprise. There are models of the City of Guangzhou and Palace of Emperor Qin Shi Huang. Some famous movies and TV series including *The Opium War* and *Jing Ke Kills the King of Qin* were shot here.

### 横店影视城

东阳横店为全国乡镇企业示范区，影视城规模浩大，人工建有广州城、秦皇宫等影视景观，曾在此拍摄过《鸦片战争》、《荆轲刺秦王》等著名影视剧。

**Tea Plantation at Longjing**

Longjing green tea, known as the "King of Green Tea," is a famous specialty of Hangzhou. It is produced in the mountains of Longjing, beside the West Lake. It has a green color, fragrant smell, sweet taste, and the leaves are shaped like sparrows tongues.

龙井茶园

龙井茶是杭州著名特产，中国绿茶之王，色泽翠绿，香郁若兰，味醇甘鲜，形似雀舌，产于西湖龙井周围群山之中

**Dragon Boat Festival at Jiangcun Village**
The Dragon Boat Festival is held on the fifth day of
the third month by the lunar calendar every year.
Emperor Qianlong of the Qing Dynasty (1644-1911)
once came to view the race and wrote a poem about it,
granting the name "Dragon Boat Festral."

**蒋村龙舟胜会**
每年农历五月初五端午节举行，历史悠久。清帝乾隆
曾亲临观赏、作诗记颂，并钦定为"龙舟胜会"。

## Shaoxing Opera

Watching operas is popular in Shaoxing. The stage is constructed by the water. Part of the audience views the opera from boats.

## 绍兴社戏

绍兴水乡看戏习俗，戏台临水搭建，每逢演社戏时，岸上挤满观众；水中泊满船只，人们在船上观戏。

## Raising Silkworms

Silkworms are raised on the Hangjia Lake Plain, which has a mild climate and fertile soil.

### 蚕桑农事

杭嘉湖平原河道如网，气候温润，土地肥腴、桑林披野，蚕事兴盛。蚕桑季节，村村采桑、养蚕、摘茧、运茧，好一幅丝绸之府风情图。

### Silkworm Festival

The Silkworm Festival at Hanshan Hill in Huzhou is held once every Pure Brightness Festival, in April. Girls make silkworm flowers of silk to pray for a bumper silk harvest. The picture shows buns made especially for the festival.

### 蚕花节

湖州含山蚕花节源于蚕花庙会，每年清明节，蚕乡的蚕娘们都要赶上含山，把绢制的蚕花带回家，以求蚕事兴旺。上图为专门为蚕花节制做蚕花团子

### Silkworm Trading Market

Silkworm breeders from all over the area sell silkworm cocoons here.

### 蚕桑交易市场

蚕农经历数月辛劳，将收获的蚕茧运至交易市场出售，蚕茧市场喜气洋洋。

**Ancient Houses in Western Zhejiang Province**

There are many houses dating from the Ming and Qing dynasties (1368-1911) in Jiande, Lanxi and Quzhou in western Zhejiang, and Jinhua in central Zhejiang. Most of them were constructed in harmony with the topography. They are made of bricks and wood decorated with wood, brick and stone carvings.

浙西古民居

浙西建德、兰溪、衢州和浙中金华一带，明清古民居甚多，一般依山傍水，因地制宜，与环境融为一体。并多为砖木结构，其中木雕、砖雕、石雕等装饰极为考究。

## Anchang Old Town

This is a district of Shaoxing with a history of over 1,000 years. The corridors, streets and markets are laid out in harmony, full of the flavor of a waterside township in southern China.

## 安昌古镇

为绍兴千年古镇，其沿河廊街已有 500 年历史。建筑古朴，廊、街、市融为一体，别具江南水乡风情。

**Longmen Old Town**

Located in Fuyang, Hangzhou, Longmen was founded by
the descendants of Sun Quan (reigned 222-252) of the Wu
Kingdom. The halls and rooms, dating from the Ming and
Qing dynasties (1368-1911), are like a maze. The picture
shows a primary school inside the old building.

龙门古镇

位于杭州富阳，系三国吴帝孙权（公元222-252年在位）
后裔聚居地，现存明清古建筑中厅屋环绕如迷宫。图为古
建筑内的小学校。

## Fisherfolks' Wedding Ceremony on the Xin'an River

After Chen Youliang, leader of an uprising in the 14th century, was defeated, nine families of his followers fled to live on the water. Gradually, they developed their own lifestyle, including a unique wedding ceremony.

### 新安江九姓渔民婚礼

14世纪陈友谅所率起义军战败后以陈姓为首的九姓被赶到新安江水上生活，不得上岸，遂形成独特的水上生活方式与婚礼形式。

**Folklore of She Township**
Jingning County, Lishui City, is the only She Autonomous County in China. The She people have their own language and folklore.

畲乡风情
丽水市景宁县是中国唯一的畲族自治县。畲族有自己独特的语言与风俗习惯，服饰特异，能歌善舞。

**Dragon Dance at the Lantern Festival**
This dance is popular in Dongyang, Longquan and Zhuji. The body of the dragon is composed of dozens or even hundreds of wooden planks.

元宵节板龙舞
流行于东阳、龙泉、诸暨一带的龙灯舞，龙身由几十乃至几百块长木板连接，可作各种盘游活动，简单朴素，别具特色。

**图书在版编目（CIP）数据**

杭州：英、汉对照 / 兰佩瑾编 . −北京：外文出版社，2001.1
ISBN 7-119-02825-1

Ⅰ．杭… Ⅱ．兰… Ⅲ．名胜古迹 − 杭州市 − 图集 Ⅳ．K928.705.51−64

中国版本图书馆 CIP 数据核字(2001)第 00337 号

**Edited by:** Lan Peijin
**Text by:** Chen Mingzhao
**Photos by:** Chen Hailin  Chu Xiaoqing  Gao Ye
Gong Weijian  Hong Jian  Hu Xiaoyang
Huang Caixiang  Lan Peijin  Liang Gang
Miao Jun  Pan Baomu  Oian Zhengjun
Shen Bin  Sun Jianping  Sun Yongxue
Wang Jianwei  Xie Guanghui
Xing Dongwen  Yan Bingyuan
Zeng Linghong  Zhang Keqing
Zhu Xiaoming, etc.
**Translated by:** Ren Ying
**Designed by:** Yuan Qing
**Executive Editor:** Lan Peijin

First Edition 2001
Third Printing 2004

**Hangzhou**

ISBN 7-119-02825-1

© Foreign Languages Press
Published by Foreign Languages Press
24 Baiwanzhuang Road, Beijing 100037, China
Home Page: http://www.flp.com.cn
E-mail Addresses: info @ flp.com.cn
sales @ flp.com.cn
*Printed in the People's Republic of China*

编辑：兰佩瑾
撰文：陈明钊
摄影：张克庆  高  昈  严炳源  沈  斌  陈海霖
苗  军  曾令洪  孙建平  胡晓阳  朱晓明
潘宝木  洪  建  龚威建  梁  刚  谢光辉
汪建伟  钱正君  黄才祥  邢东文  孙永学
兰佩瑾  初小青等
翻译：任  瑛
设计：元  青
责任编辑：兰佩瑾

**杭  州**

兰佩瑾  编

© 外文出版社
外文出版社出版
（中国北京百万庄大街24号）
邮政编码：100037
外文出版社网页：http://www.flp.com.cn
外文出版社电子邮件地址：info @ flp.com.cn
sales @ flp.com.cn
天时印刷 (深圳) 有限公司印刷
北京骏马行图文中心制作
2001年(24开)第一版
2004 年第一版第三次印刷
（英汉）
ISBN 7-119-02825-1/J·1556（外）
004800（精）